BERWOTA98

Wonders
of the Antarctic

DODD, MEAD WONDER BOOKS

Wonders
of the Antarctic

by JACQUELYN BERRILL

ILLUSTRATED BY THE AUTHOR

DODD, MEAD & COMPANY

New York 1958

TO MY VERY GROWN-UP CHILDREN
    ELSILYN
        PEGGY
            MICHAEL
May they never grow too old to wonder —

Contents

Wonders
of the Antarctic

South Polar Lands

Do you know where you live? I can hear you laugh as you answer, "Of course, I know my address." If you know it exactly, it might be something like this:

Name: Bob (or Jane) Smith
Street: 1 Main Street
City: Jackson
County: Lincoln
State: Ohio
Country: United States of America
Hemisphere: Western Hemisphere
Planet: Earth

You could stick a pin in the exact spot where your home town is located on a map of the Western Hemisphere like this:

If your address is in the Eastern Hemisphere, then you are just as familiar with this map and can easily locate your home.

But these show only two of the ways of looking at the Earth. There are others as well. If you are an Eskimo or a Laplander, for instance, you can find your home on this view of the top of our earth, for you live somewhere around the North Pole.

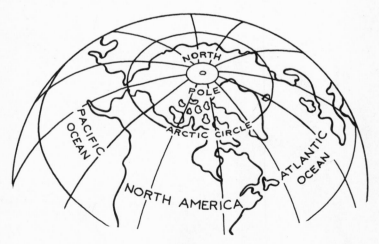

If you were a King Penguin, your homeland would be found on the underside of the globe — at the bottom of the world.

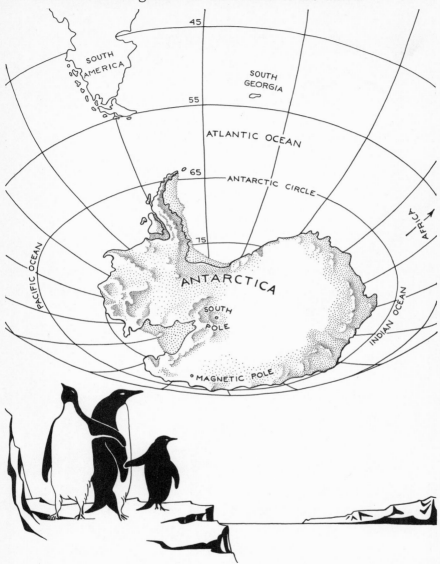

This is a strange view of the world, isn't it? Strange from our viewpoint but not strange at all to the penguin.

No boys and girls can give Antarctica as a part of their address. No child was ever born on this southern continent — no child has ever lived there. Only animals that are especially fitted to survive in cold climates live in the frozen southland. The Antarctic continent is the coldest place on earth, with temperatures recorded of more than one hundred degrees below zero. Don't you wonder how any creature can stand such cold?

Please don't get the idea, from the last map, that you are looking at a small island of floating ice, for Antarctica is not that at all. What you actually see is a continent of six million square miles of land — almost as large as the United States of America and Europe put together. Perhaps this sketch will show you how large it really is.

The land is covered with a thick sheet of ice, except where mountains, some as high as fifteen thousand feet, pierce the landscape. And you mustn't think the land is low, for the South Pole itself is situated on a ten-thousand-foot high plateau or table-land.

Not only is Antarctica extremely cold but, in the wintertime, wind blows from ninety to two hundred miles per hour over the

Adelie coast, with a force as strong as a hurricane. The cause of this was a mystery for a long time. Exploration by aircraft was necessary to discover a great, sloping trough, two hundred to three hundred miles wide, lying between a high mountain range and a dome of ice and extending from the coast all the way to the South Pole. In the winter, when the high interior of Antarctica becomes intensely cold, the heavy, frigid air flows down this trough like water down a chute. Of course, some of it spills through gaps in the mountains but most of it goes all the way to the coast, gaining enormous speed and spreading over the sea as a howling Antarctic gale.

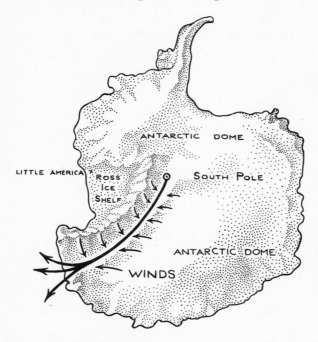

Suppose you wish to find this frozen continent from the address you gave me a moment ago. If you live in the Western Hemisphere, you would travel south to the tip of South America. If you live in the Eastern Hemisphere, you would go south to the Cape of Good

Hope, or perhaps to the south side of Australia. From these familiar places let us have a look at the bottom of the world.

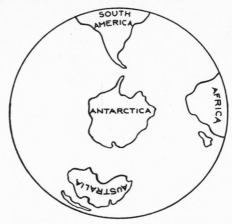

Perhaps you had better stop for a while and learn a little more about this South Polar continent before you venture in your imagination any nearer. You would not like this cold land, where for half the year the sun never comes above the horizon and all is dark, while the other part of the year is one long day and the sun does not sink out of sight at all. Not a single tree or flower is to be seen there — no cities, no towns, no permanent settlements as we know them. The only human visitors are whalers who come during the long day to catch whales and leave when the bright season is over, and scientists who come for short periods to study weather conditions, animals, or the land itself. This South Polar land is not attractive to men, for all but about one hundred square miles of it is permanently covered with ice eight thousand feet or more thick.

This great deep ice cap forms glaciers which move slowly toward the sea, where they become walls or cliffs, fifty to two hundred feet high, all along the coast. Around the edge of this cold land is a great floating sheet of ice, anchored to the shore. The largest of these

16

ice sheets, the Ross Barrier, is about as big as France and is made of ice five hundred to fifteen hundred feet thick. Chips many miles long break off with thundering noises and float away. When this happens, the glaciers are said to be "calving." Once loose, the icebergs then start to float west and north, where they eventually reach warmer water. Carved by the waves and wind into fantastic shapes that are often like palaces or cathedrals, they break up into smaller icebergs and finally melt away.

When you are standing on the tip of one of the Southern Hemisphere continents, you are looking toward Antarctica across six hundred miles or more of the roughest seas in the world. There are no islands of any size in all that vast stretch of water around the South Polar lands. The winds blow continuously from the west, whipping the ocean waves to fantastic heights. Overhead the Wandering Albatross sails before the winds and circles around the continent at the bottom of the world.

It never rains in Antarctica — all the water comes down in the form of snow, to be caught up by the strong winds and blown about in great blizzards that last for days. No wonder there are no trees and that the only plants are mosses and lichens that cling to the rocks.

There is no disease in Antarctica — the air is sterilized by ultraviolet rays (those invisible rays of the sun that give you a sunburn). Nor is there dust or rust or soot. When modern explorers visit a hut abandoned by early adventurers, they find the wood like new, the nails bright and even the food left behind still fit to be eaten. This land is really like a vast deep-freeze, where time stands still and nothing spoils.

Under all the white hard snow and the blue-green ice, the land is known to be rich in minerals, even coal. Since these deposits were made by ancient forests of tree-ferns that could only grow in tropical climates, the presence of coal at the South Pole is one of the great mysteries that scientists are trying to solve. Was it once warm at the South Pole, a long time ago, or has the crust of the earth been sliding slowly about? Was the land now beneath the Antarctic ice once in a warmer region?

If you were to cross those rough southernmost seas, dodging the icebergs, to land at last on the great sheet of ice, you would become confused, for the sunlight gleaming on the snow and clouds creates a white light everywhere in which landmarks and shadows disappear. A companion standing near you may seem to vanish and then reappear a moment later. Your ship may look upside-down in the sky and the sun may seem to rise and fall many times a day. Mountains far away appear to be close, and a rough piece of ice may loom as high as a steeple.

When the sun is low, the sky takes on a greenish tinge. Suddenly, a veil of intense blueness covers the land — and is just as suddenly lifted. All of these illusions are created by the light passing through dry and dust-free atmosphere, but they seem real and you think you are "seeing things."

The seas surrounding the continent are not only the roughest but the richest in the world — they teem with life. And where sea food is plentiful, birds are abundant; and seals and whales, the only mammals to brave the icy waters, come to feed. Also, many animals find they can safely raise their young where food is so easily obtained. Some have even adapted to the cold to such an extent that they can spend all the year in or about the icy continent at the bottom of the world.

Summer and
the Adelie Penguins

Who will be on hand to welcome you to Antarctica, if in your mind you cross those stormy waters to the frozen land? The same "inhabitants" who welcomed the early explorers and whalers — the penguins! These curious birds belong to this cold climate, or perhaps it would be more correct to say Anarctica belongs to the penguins, especially the Emperor and the Adelie Penguins who spend their lives on and around this icy continent.

You would have to make your trip in the southern summer, which is at the same time of year as the northern winter, in order to have the sun shining so that you could see even the black and white penguins. You probably know that the summer day and the winter night become longer as you approach Antarctica, and once you have

Adelie Penguins welcome you eagerly, lose interest and go about their business.

crossed the Antarctic Circle, which is drawn around the South Pole at a distance of 23½°, you will find continuous daylight at mid-summer and unbroken darkness in mid-winter. If you should continue as far as the South Pole, these periods of dark and light would lengthen until you would find only one "day" a year, with six months of daylight and one "night" with six months of darkness. Spring in Antarctica begins in September, and summer in November.

You would find that the small Adelie Penguins had already arrived and were waiting to greet you, just as they did a French explorer over a hundred years ago who named the shoreline and its penguin inhabitants after his wife Adelie.

The Adelies have as much curiosity in people as people have in birds, so they waddle toward you eagerly, with their black tails dragging in the snow. Completely unafraid of you, they approach boldly and stop about a yard away to stare at you curiously, first with one eye and then the other. You can't help laughing, for these black and white birds remind you of nothing so much as little gentlemen all dressed for a party in their formal evening clothes. You can't even tell them apart, for males and females look exactly alike. They see nothing to bother them and soon lose interest, so they stretch and yawn and turn their backs on you and move away with their "coat-tails" making tracks in the snow. But they have important business to attend to, or so it seems.

Let us go back a few months, to find out where these inquisitive birds have been and how they have managed to arrive here across the icy water, and just what is their "important business?"

All the dark winter months, the small Adelie Penguins have lived on the floating ice pack that was moving to the west and north toward warmer waters. For months they have done nothing but swim and fish and rest on the moving ice. But now it is spring, and the long polar night is over, and it is time for them to travel south to the nearest land, in order to make their nests and raise penguin chicks.

The cock penguin never walks far to get a stone if he can find one near at hand!

Leaving the icebergs and the pack ice to continue drifting north and finally to break up and melt in warmer waters, the penguins begin to swim southward. This is sometimes a journey of five hundred miles, and they have to swim all that distance because present-day penguins cannot fly in the air. Once they used their wings as other birds do, but that was long ago. Today, penguin wings are too short to raise their heavy bodies into the air. The wings have changed to flippers or paddles, making a penguin perfectly fitted for water travel, for the body is streamlined like that of a fish, and with its flippers it actually flies beneath the surface, beating its "wings" against the water instead of air. The thickly packed feathers make a dry insulating coat that no cold or wet can penetrate. Even the eyes, not good for seeing out of water, are well suited to see underwater. So the bird is able to keep a sharp lookout for its chief enemy, the Leopard Seal, and to find its food. It swims deep, without making a ripple on the water, except when it takes a quick trip to the surface every so often, in order to breathe.

Yet this long water journey is only part of the trip. Once the penguin reaches the edge of the shore ice, it leaps out of the water and lands on its feet in a standing position on the ice, about five feet above the water — with several hundred miles yet to travel over snow before the breeding ground is reached.

The females arrive first. It is the duty of the female penguin to go ahead and select a nest site and get it ready. Before her stretches a long line of other female Adelies marching along over the ice in single file. She loses no time but steps into the line, following closely the footsteps of the penguin in front of her. Perhaps it is her short-sightedness that makes her stay so close to the bird ahead. She might lose her way if she didn't. We do not know how penguins find their course through the water to this ice barrier or how they get their direction across the hundreds of miles of ice with no landmarks to guide them. One penguin must be first in this long line and it is pos-sible that she is guided by the position of the sun. Nobody knows the answers to all of the questions you might ask about penguins — maybe we never will.

The penguin walks along in the single line, putting her small feet down 130 times a minute, dragging her "coattail" in the snow and leaving a trail made by the central feathers. When she comes to a small crack in the ice, she jumps over it to reach the other side. Wide crevices must be journeyed around. While she plods along, she makes a wheezing sound as if she is out of breath. When she is tired of walking, she falls forward on her breast and toboggans along, pushing with her legs and holding her head high. If she needs to hurry to catch up to the penguin in front, she pushes with her flippers as well as with her feet and in this way can travel over the ice faster than a man can run.

In the long procession of Adelies, some birds are walking and others tobogganing at the same time, but all keep in line. When it is dark, they stop to sleep until dawn but never break their formation on the journey. Each of these southbound penguins seems to have a

Skua gulls are always waiting to grab an unguarded egg or chick.

special goal, for when a rookery is reached with plenty of room to spare, a few drop out of line to make nests, while others pass by without hesitation, heading for rookeries many miles farther south and nearer the Pole.

Dinner time for the Adelie chicks

The journey may last two weeks for one of these Adelies, and by then the sharp ice will have cut her feet until there is a trail of blood left on the white snow behind her. When the desired nesting sight is near, she becomes excited, as do all the other penguins. The line formation breaks up and she flops on her breast and pushes with flippers and legs, screaming loudly as she rushes to join the others who have already arrived at the rookery site.

The most southerly of all the rookeries is the one at Cape Crozier, on the Ross Sea. Thousands of Adelie Penguins go there each summer to build their nests and raise their young. You might expect a nursery rookery to be located in a place at least partly sheltered from the fierce winds. But no, the Adelies make their nests where the wind blows strongest! Why? Because the wind blows the snow away, uncovering the pebbles on the beaches, and pebbles are the building material for the penguins' nests.

A clamor of squawking and cackling and piping is heard as the females begin to pick nesting sites in the crowded rookery. Many go directly to places they seem to recognize, for they walk right over unoccupied spots to select a special place farther on. They quarrel among themselves and strike at one another if they happen to settle too close together.

When a female has selected a place just far enough removed from her neighbors so that only their beaks can touch, she settles down to let the heat of her breast thaw the ground and snow so that she may scratch out a circular depression. Then she sits, quenching her thirst by eating snow near the nest, and waits for the males to come and pay court.

By the end of October, all the males have arrived, having followed along exactly the same path taken by the females. Although sleepy from the long trip over the ice, they try to stay awake long enough to choose their mates.

The cock walks through the rookery, eating snow and looking about. Every now and then he ruffles up his feathers and dozes for a while. Upon waking up again, he moves on until he finds a hen that pleases him. Then, if possible, he picks up a pebble in his beak and presents it to her. This seems to be the penguin way of saying "Let's build a home!" Looking a little silly, he stands in front of the female and waves his flippers and cackles. If the lady of his choice does not find him satisfactory, she pecks at him, although, being a stubborn fellow, he waits long enough to see if she is just pretending to be angry or really means it. If the pecking continues, he moves on to offer his gift pebble to another hen, this time sitting down quietly in front of her and waiting. If she accepts the gift, he moves closer and they "talk" in low sounds. After a while, they sway together from side to side with their beaks crossed, making shrill cries all the while.

Often two cocks fight for the attention of the same hen. They hit out with their flippers and beaks until one becomes exhausted and moves away. Sometimes even the Adelie hen becomes so excited that she also enters the fight, taking both sides at once!

After the courting is over, the nest building starts. The male carries stones of various sizes, all smooth and round, to the hen, who builds them into a low wall about the scooped-out nesting place. She has to guard her pile of building stones carefully; an unguarded stone will soon be put into a neighbor's nest. The cock penguin never walks far to get building material if he can pick some up close to home. If he is caught thieving, he makes himself sleek and thin and tries to get lost in the crowd of penguins as soon as possible, just like a small boy caught stealing cookies!

Soon two eggs appear in almost every nest and family life settles over the rookery — but not quiet, since there is continual bickering with the neighbors — although each pair is faithful and affectionate. So far, the birds have not eaten for more than a month. They have fasted since they began their journey south. Only now, with two eggs in the nest, can the couple give thought to food. Taking turns, one guards the eggs while the other goes fishing.

It does seem that when the penguins have traveled so far to

Penguins shoot out of the water in a hurry when a Killer Whale is anywhere near.

build their nurseries, they should at least find safety there, but this is not the case. Just as soon as the Adelies move southward, so do the South Polar skuas. These large brown gulls scratch out rough nests on the heights above the penguin rookeries, and by the time the penguin eggs are laid in November there are thousands of skuas ready and waiting to grab an unguarded egg!

The skuas have the distinction of being the most southerly nesting birds, but they also probably have the worst reputation of any birds. Into these crude nests they lay two eggs, but when the chicks, covered with blue-gray down, are hatched, the parents give them almost no protection or brooding. The young ones even have to pick up their food from the ground near the nest where the parents drop it. The baby birds quarrel loudly all the time and if one chick is pushed out of the nest, an adult skua swoops down on it and swallows it. This may also happen to unguarded penguin eggs and chicks.

If a skua even flies over the rookeries, all the Adelies join in a shrill screaming. Because penguins can't fly, there is no way to fight them off. The poor penguins just have to put up with their raids. When you add all the noise made by the skuas to the screams of the penguins, you can see that the penguin nursery is anything but quiet and peaceful.

During his first feeding after the long fast, the Adelie cock may stay away for nearly two weeks, catching and eating fish and shrimp, before he returns to take over the household duties and permit his mate to feed for an equally long period. After that first long fishing expedition, the couple take turns feeding each day, all through the incubating period of about five weeks.

Whenever the cock penguin takes his turn at sitting on the eggs, he does nothing more than keep them warm, and he is always ready to leave them to pick a fight with a neighbor. The hen, however, takes her responsibilities more seriously. She cuddles and clucks and turns the eggs carefully at intervals. Although she may quarrel with the hen next door, she never leaves the nest to do so.

When the time comes to change guard, the sitter seems to want to stay put and there is a great deal of "discussion." Finally, the sitter stands, the two penguins rub necks on both sides and cackle softly. The newcomer is then allowed to see the eggs and touch them and finally to settle down over them.

As the ground becomes wet with the melting snow, the cock brings more pebbles to raise the level of the nest higher and higher. He also brings chunks of snow for his mate to eat when all the snow nearby is melted. She seems to like his gifts of snow, which she eats to quench her thirst.

Snow Petrels come to this cold part of the world because of the abundant food in the seas.

At long last there are two helpless, downy-gray babies in the nest, with black heads and faces, each weighing about two and one half ounces. The parents' stomachs then bulge with the food they bring to the nestlings. When feeding the chicks, they bend over so far that their heads turn upside down so that the little ones may eat out of their mouths, as though out of a trough. When the baby birds are stronger and can stand in the nest, they feed directly from the beaks of the adults.

29

After twelve days, the young weigh about two and a half pounds, so you can see that they get plenty of food, especially small fish and shrimp. The journey to the water and back is usually a long one and may be very steep. Even when, as in some rookeries, the penguin has to climb nine hundred feet to reach the nest (and it may take him twenty-four hours to make two trips) the babies seem to get food enough and grow fast.

About the middle of January, when the penguin chicks are half-grown, they join up with other chicks in the nurseries to form groups of about a dozen to twenty. A few old birds then take over the guard duty as nurses, leaving the other adults free to go fishing.

Thus freed, the parents join the other off-duty adults on the edge of the ice. Here they chase one another and chatter and appear to enjoy their new freedom from their responsibilities. Most of the time these adult penguins seem to have but one aim — that of making someone else take the first plunge into the icy waters. Of course, each one is reluctant, not because the water is cold but because a Leopard Seal may be waiting under the ice for a penguin dinner. There is a great deal of pushing — and finally one bird goes overboard. The other penguins wait a minute to see if the bird is safe. If there is no trouble, they follow as quickly as possible, rolling and splashing and making deep dives. Then they climb out on the already crowded floating ice cakes, and as they squeeze on from behind, they push others off the front and the fun starts all over again.

When their play is over and they are full of the small shrimps called krill, or when a Sea Leopard is near, the Adelies head for the ice, come above the surface twenty to forty yards away, to get their bearings, and then dive for the ice. They pop up about a yard from the edge, like a jack-in-the-box, and land on the ice in a standing position. Once safe, the penguins chat and rest a while before they start walking back toward the rookery.

Each adult full of food goes straight to the nursery where the chicks are kept and feeds the hungry ones. Is it his or her own chick the parent feeds? We do not know. Perhaps the one that is yelling the loudest is fed first. Finally all the chicks are satisfied, since many adults are on feeding duty.

It may be summer, but the Antarctic summer, although continually light and sometimes warm enough for a man to work stripped to the waist, is often very cold. During an October storm the temperature may drop to 43° below zero. The entire rookery becomes covered with snow. Returning cocks are greatly disturbed to find only the beaks of their mates appearing above the drifts. In a blizzard, the penguins turn their backs to the wind and their feathers become filled with snow. A group of young in a nursery will crowd close, with their heads together in the center, until the storm passes.

As soon as their down has changed to feathers, the chicks are ready to take to the water. They do not need to learn how to swim but they are reluctant to make the first jump. The old birds try to tempt them to take the plunge by paddling up to shallow water and calling and calling. The young chicks still stand far back from the edge and beg for food, but the parents do not bring any more krill to them and the young are slowly coaxed to "come and get it."

Although the skua is always a menace to young penguins, there are other and less dangerous birds nesting near the rookeries. The Antarctic Petrels, for instance — beautiful brown birds with a broad white cross on their wings — fly constantly over the rookery to and from their own nesting grounds. These birds have come to the South Polar land because the food in the sea close by is plentiful. Here in their nests, huddled close together on the cliffs, they raise their young.

The petrels fish in the same waters as the Adelies, for they, too, live on the small shrimp — so abundant in these icy waters. They also

31

spend many hours on the same icebergs with the penguins, squatting in clusters, resting and digesting their food. The Antarctic sun soon fades their coats to buff, but with each autumn moult, or renewal of feathers, their natural beauty is again restored!

Then there is the Snow Petrel, the daintiest bird in the Antarctic. It is pure satiny-white — as you'd expect from its name — and small like a tern. Over and among the feeding Adelie Penguins, great flocks of Snow Petrels fly close together, as though they were all one bird — all of them turning and twisting at the same time. Flocks of these same birds have given many an explorer warning of an iceberg not far away, for it is well known that where the Snow Petrels are, there are sure to be bergs or pack ice. All around the Antarctic continent, these pure white birds add their cries to those of the other breeding birds. In fact, their cries are heard far into the night, long after other birds have settled down to rest.

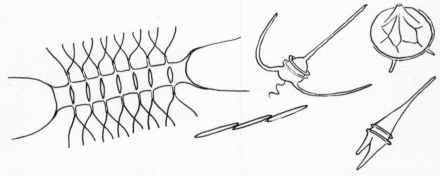

The cold water is filled with tiny plants and animals called plankton.

Snow Petrels have also come to this cold part of the world because of the abundant food. The cold Antarctic waters well upward, rich in fertilizing minerals upon which tiny plants and animals, called plankton, thrive. Larger sea animals like the small shrimp or "krill," live, in turn, upon these little plants and animals and become so abundant themselves that the sea seems almost like soup at times. Larger fish live on krill, as do the penguins and petrels and other Antarctic birds — and so also do the seals and even the largest whales.

The Crab-eater Seals, however, pay no attention to the penguins feeding in the waters near the icy shores, for they are interested mainly in the sea creatures that live on the bottom, particularly the crabs. The seals dive to the sea floor and scoop up sand and crabs, using their teeth as sieves to eject the water and sand, but retaining the crabs, together with a few stones, to help the stomach break up the hard crab shells.

Because fish and squid are so abundant in the waters along these far southern shores, the Weddell Seal finds life satisfactory all the year round. Wherever the ice is weak enough to be cut through by the seals, so as to provide air holes, these blue-gray animals, with their dark and light irregular spots and white whiskers on the soft

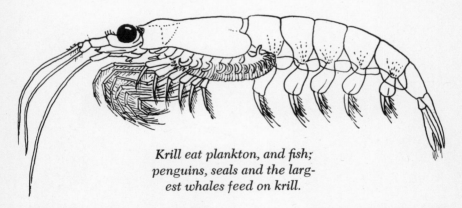

Krill eat plankton, and fish; penguins, seals and the largest whales feed on krill.

pads of their upper lips, climb out onto the ice and look about with their enormous eyes set in their small faces. The terribly low temperature of the winter night often causes them to take refuge in the water under the ice, which never drops below 28° above zero. By keeping their breathing holes open, the Weddell Seals can stay underwater

33

like this for long periods. Sometimes colonies of Weddells live five miles or more from open water and depend upon a chain of blow holes in the ice serving as air filling stations along a well-defined route, at about one-hundred-and-eighty-yard intervals. A seal can therefore swim for long distances under the ice, stopping at frequent airholes to breathe. Since about every third hole is a large one, the animal can climb out onto the protecting ice if he feels there is a Killer Whale, his chief enemy, anywhere near in the water.

The Adelies may see Weddell Seals rolled over on their backs asleep on the ice, or they may meet them while fishing in the same waters, but they pass by without fear, for these seals, like the Crab-eaters, are not enemies but, instead, share their same common foes.

Penguins are not afraid of the Weddell Seals who cut breathing holes in the ice with their teeth.

The Leopard Seal, however, is a dreaded enemy of the penguin and the other Antarctic birds. These seals have spots like leopards and hunt as fiercely as leopards do on land. They feed upon the krill eaters — penguins, fish and petrels. They stalk their prey alone and are savage, waiting stealthily under the ice edge to catch any animal that is careless. The Adelie Penguins are always on guard when fishing or diving, for they know that this spotted seal with the long body and neck has a large mouth with very sharp teeth!

When the Leopard Seal is full and satisfied, it swims at a great speed toward the ice floe, breaks surface and shoots out of the water like a rocket. It usually lands about six feet from the edge of the ice, rolls on its side, folds its flippers on its chest and goes to sleep. Only then are the penguins safe!

About the time when the penguin chicks have lost their down and have grown a new coat of blue-black feathers and can go into the water if they will, the adults begin to moult, too. From this time on, the parents and the old nurses desert the young, who must then live on their fat until they become hungry enough to enter the water and discover that they, too, are able to catch their own food.

By February, the Antarctic summer is about over and darkness is closing in. Ice is forming all along the shore and stretching far out to sea. The Adelies, adult and young together, start on their journey north and fall into single line, marching toward the open water. They leave the shores of the continent they have used for raising their young and for changing their coat of feathers. They travel hundreds of miles to the edge of the ice packs, where they dive and fish and play from March until August, while the dark closes in over the continent they have left behind. When another Antarctic summer comes along, the adult Adelie Penguins will again make the long journey by sea and over the ice to reach the familiar rookeries and will again produce another generation of penguins.

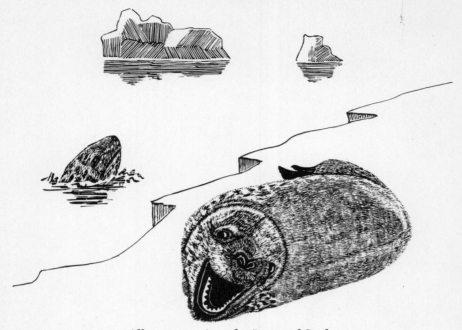

All penguins fear the Leopard Seals.

If your visit to Antarctica was real and not imaginary, I know you would agree with the explorers that the penguin "people" who inhabit this continent are most charming. Perhaps you would also call them, as they do, "the clowns of the Antarctic."

Winter and
the Emperor of Antarctica

When all the birds that have used Antarctica as a breeding and feeding ground have flown north again to warmer climates, and all the little Adelie Penguins have marched in single file northward to the edge of the pack ice; when the period of sunlight becomes shorter and shorter and temperatures drop to forty or more degrees below zero, the real "Emperors" of the frozen continent begin to arrive.

The Emperor Penguin is rightly named, for it is the tallest and most beautiful of the many kinds of penguins that live on and around the land at the bottom of the world. This penguin stands as high as a man's chest, and he wears a dress suit so black that it appears dark bluish. On each side of the neck, this brilliantly black and white bird has bright yellow-orange areas. Most strikingly dressed, he is!

All around the continent, at the beginning of the long, dark Antarctic winter, these large birds shoot up from the depths of the ice-filled waters and land on the ice shelf several feet from the edge. This is the end of their long migration of hundreds of miles through icy waters to their breeding grounds on the South Polar land. How the Emperor Penguins get their direction through the black waters of almost uniform temperatures and saltiness is a mystery no one has yet solved. They cannot see or smell or feel their way to these icy shores. Why they come to the coldest place on earth to raise their young in the dark is still another mystery.

If you are ready for another imaginary trip, look at the map on page 88. Find the rookery of the Emperor Penguins on the west end of the Ross shelf ice. There are many such rookeries around the continent. This one has about seven thousand birds, all crowded close together in the dark. It is called Cape Crozier.

It is April and very cold, but the plump Emperors do not seem to mind, for their layers of blubber serve as a protection against such low temperatures. Their bills, flippers and feet are smaller than would be expected on a heavy bird weighing as much as seventy pounds, but this means, of course, that there is less of these unpadded areas to get cold. The penguin needs a large amount of food to give it energy to plunge into the cold Antarctic waters. Fortunately, the capacity for producing and storing this bodily heat and energy is very high.

The Emperor Penguins cling to the ways of their ancestors as they travel over the same old trails to familiar rookeries, even if those trails cross the roughest ground — or ice — and a new and easier and safer route is right before their eyes. But the penguin is nearsighted, which may account for the apparent lack of awareness. A newly-arrived bird joins hundreds of others, each of which looks exactly like the rest, in a rookery nursery situated near a wide crack in the sea-ice. It is important for Emperors to live near open water where food may be secured. The winds continually widen the cracks by forcing the ice fields to move northward into the Ross Sea.

The Emperor walks with great dignity upright on the ice, although when in a hurry he drops on his breast and toboggans rapidly by pushing with the powerful legs and flippers. This penguin is no more intelligent than others — he just looks more so! He is aloof and curious and sociable at the same time, and the absence of eyebrows adds a comical and quizzical expression as well.

38

Emperors walk with dignity upright on the ice, although when in a hurry they drop on their breasts and toboggan rapidly by pushing with their legs and flippers.

Little is actually known about the courtship of the Emperor Penguins because of the difficulties of observing in the darkness and cold. In this bitter darkness, men have heard their loud metallic trumpeting — much louder and more musical than the voice of the

The courtship of the Emperor Penguins takes place in the bitterly cold dark winter.

Adelie — which carries for miles over the ice floes. The call is given with the head erect. First, there is a cackling and chattering and a musical note uttered with the head low on the breast, as all the air is expelled. The trumpet note comes as the lungs are filled with air again. If you can imagine what several thousand penguins sound like, all cackling at the same time, you will have some idea of the uproar going on in the penguin nursery.

Above the rookery strange lights sometimes flash across the northern sky. The curtains of color start around the Magnetic Pole and spread slowly in all directions, or change rapidly from shades of blue to red and violet in quick succession. These heavenly lights, called "Southern Lights" (perhaps you have seen the somewhat similar "Northern Lights" on a clear, cold winter night) are caused by sun particles traveling very rapidly into earth's atmosphere.

In June, when the temperatures are from eighty to one hundred degrees below zero, and the wind blows the snow about in blizzards most of the time, when the only light in the continual blackness is from the stars or the "Southern Lights," the single Emperor Penguin egg is laid. The large, pale-green, rough egg, weighing about a pound, is held constantly in the space between the belly, tail, and feet. If it touched the ice even for a moment, the chick inside the shell would freeze. The adult bird squats with upturned toes and depressed tail, and a broad fold of skin covers the egg as it rests on the feet.

The precious egg must be kept warm constantly, and it is shifted from one adult bird to another without ever letting it touch the ice. Only a fraction of these Emperor Penguins breed during any one winter, but all have a warm pouch and a warm heart for any exposed egg or chick. The whole community, not just the mated pairs, feels broody, which is a good thing, for without the co-operation of all the mature birds, the baby penguins might perish. As it is, the combined adults manage to raise enough baby chicks each dark winter to maintain the Emperor population. By sharing the business of incubating the eggs, they find more time for securing food.

You may wonder how the penguins find their food in the inky black waters. Do they see the small shrimp or smell them or feel the tiny animals in the water? We do not know, but we do know that this amazing bird is as efficient in water as any other water creature. As well as having a streamlined shape for swift water travel and strong flippers for "flying" through water, the penguins have eyes for looking upward without raising the head, so that they can see above them in the water and keep a sharp watch for the Leopard Seal, their chief enemy.

For seven or eight weeks, the Emperor Penguin shuffles over the ice, and you would never know there was an egg being carried along, too. If she trips and falls, she tumbles like a stiff statue, with the egg still held tightly in place. By using her bill as a prop and by bracing with her flippers, she can recover her erect position without losing her precious egg.

The instinct to brood is greatest when the bird is full of food, although by the time her mate returns, filled with krill, he finds her hungry and ready to have him take over the job of nursing. The egg is then carefully rolled from one warm space to the other without chilling the chick within, which may be almost ready to crack the shell.

The chick is finally hatched out, all dressed up in a gray down coat, but with a black head and pure white around the eyes, cheeks and throat. The baby is kept just as safely inside the warm pouch as the egg had been — and it is just as carefully guarded from the cold as it is shifted from one adult to another. At first, the chick grows slowly, but there is a constant peeping of four notes which some say sound like "give-me-some-more," "give-me-some-more," and perhaps

42

that is exactly what it does mean! The chick opens its mouth and prepares to swallow whenever its bill is touched. Then it thrusts out the head to take food from the turned-down mouth of the parent.

Sometimes the chick sits for a while "outside" on the feet of the adult, backed close against the warm sheltering breast, and at other times the baby sits on the ice and tucks his head into the "warming chamber." After two months, there is a spurt of growth, and by the time the chick is four months old and has grown a second coat of darker gray, it reaches up to the shoulders of the adults.

By October, the Emperor Penguins become restless and unsettled. A wind storm from the north jams the ice at the head of the Ross Sea against the shores, and then the wind changes, which starts the ice floes moving. This is the signal for all of the free, unemployed penguins to march in single file across the ice to the very edge, where they crowd together, waiting for their ice raft to break away and start to take them on their long journey northward. The last to leave are the parents with young, but as time passes they, too, fall into line. Presently all the Emperor Penguins have left the rookeries and are moving northward on large floating rafts of ice.

The young cannot swim until they have completed their moults — that is, until they have lost their downy coats and replaced them with coats of bluish-gray feathers — so the parents must continue to feed the chicks. There is a race to complete this change before the ice breaks up into small pieces, forcing the young birds into the water to swim and feed for themselves.

The adults spend most of the last weeks on the ice raft feeding themselves in preparation for the long fast they must endure while they, too, change their feathers. They leave the ice raft with the young still aboard and start swimming southward again, to a more stable place, where the ice is still fastened tightly to the shore. They

*The chick sits for a while 'outside' on the
feet of the adult.*

shoot out of the water and crowd together on the pack. Here they
must wait patiently for their new feather coats to grow, for until they
are ready the birds dare not enter the cold waters to feed.

By January, there are thousands of moulting birds on the east end
of the Ross shelf ice. Sometimes the piece of ice they are on breaks
off and is carried out to sea, with the helpless birds sitting and waiting. If they are lucky, the moult is completed before the ice cake
breaks up, and they can slip into the water to find food and once
again swim southward toward the breeding ground, to spend another
long winter night.

But what about the young we left on the ice floes drifting northward? The young penguins stay around the pack ice, swimming and
playing and watching out for the Leopard Seals for a year and a half.
Then they, too, swim to the continental shore ice, to change their
faded coats for the regal black and white and orange suits of the
Emperor of the Antarctic before they make their first journey to the
rookery nursery, to raise more Emperor Penguins in their turn.

Landbase for Antarctic Birds

All around the South Polar continent a belt of very strong winds blows from west to east with almost nothing to obstruct their force. They are indescribably fierce. Can you find 40° south latitude on the map? Someone has called the latitudes in this part of the world the "Roaring Forties, Furious Fifties and Shrieking Sixties." In the "Furious Fifties" of the South Atlantic region, you will find South Georgia Island. For much of the year, giant icebergs fill the waters around it and several feet of snow cover the land, except during the brief period of Antarctic summer when the sun melts the snow along the shore of the island. The mountains continue to lie under a blanket of snow and ice throughout the year.

Birds that fly above the South Polar seas need a land base on which to make their nests and raise their young, and seals that swim in the ice-filled waters must have a home on solid ground on which to give birth to and suckle their pups. The islands in this part of the world are very much alive during the summer months, and it is to South Georgia Island we are going next in our imaginary journey. We might have chosen any one of several other islands, but we will go to South Georgia because it is one of the few whose shores humans have found it possible to reach.

South Georgia is about a hundred miles long and thirty miles across. Bays and fjords cut far inland, while snow-covered foothills rise to three or four hundred feet, with ice-capped mountains towering nine thousand feet above. Glaciers fill all the valleys, and two of them, larger than the rest, move down toward the south shore. One glacier pushes rocks before it, to form a large moraine, and the other ends in a cliff of ice a hundred feet above the sea. Great pieces of ice are continually breaking off or "calving" and sending thousands of tons of ice cascading into the ocean with a thunderous sound. Blizzards and gales sweep furiously over the island, and fog often hides it from sight. Only rarely is there good weather. Of course, people do not live here permanently but for brief periods only, when whaling

King Penguins have a good look for the Leopard Seal before they go swimming.

46

Penguins spend much time preening their feathers.

stations are set up as headquarters on the shores. The whalers leave as soon as their work is done.

Along the shores and foothills of South Georgia, a coarse grass, called tussock, grows in clumps. Each spring, the season's new growth comes forth from the old stumps of the previous summer season, so that in time the tufts become very high and the roots thick and matted. When the winter snow melts, the water runs off between the plants, carrying away the dirt and cutting deep channels which are used as highways by the penguins on their way to their rookeries. Can you picture all this in your mind? Tussocks growing, plant on plant, and becoming higher and higher, with deeper and deeper excavating taking place. At last, the only earth left in place is held together by the fibrous roots of the great grass whose long blades meet overhead, like a jungle, while Elephant Seals wallow in the mud beneath.

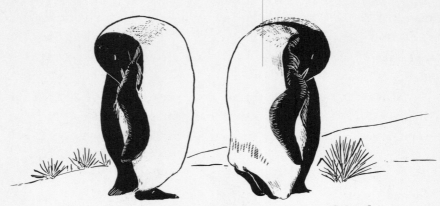

Sleeping. The bird on the right is resting on his tail.

South Georgia is a sanctuary for many creatures during their breeding period: albatrosses, petrels, penguins, and seals. The smaller breeding birds use the tussock grass and roots for nesting materials, or hide their nests in the clumps, or even burrow into the dirt among the roots for greater safety. All around the shores, the water is so filled with krill that it seems almost like soup. Large and small fish and squid, and even jellyfish a yard across, are abundant. There is

Fights are easily started in the rookery and soon all join in the fun. The king on the left is turning her egg.

plenty of food and good shelter, and some creatures have found that the island provides their needs so well that they do not have to migrate to warmer climates but spend the whole year on or close to the island.

This is the way with the King Penguins, those curious birds only slightly smaller than the Emperor and just as fascinating. It is a real wonder there are any Kings left on South Georgia to welcome you,

Chicks almost grown are still fed by adults.

for these little fellows are extremely friendly and can easily be caught. Whalers and explorers alike have killed the Kings for their beautiful feather-skins and their stored-up fat, and have gathered their eggs because they found them good eating.

The King Penguins walk in single file along the channels between the clumps of tussock grass until they reach the bare moraines or ridges well back from the water. By the side of a snow bank with a glacial torrent, exposed to constantly blowing winds and chilled by the snow of the higher slopes, the Kings build their rookery. Here they crowd close together, and the territory each can defend with its flippers becomes its own special place to fight over.

The single egg is incubated in the same manner as the Emperor's egg: on top of the feet and under a flap of skin forming a brood pouch.

Like their relatives, the Adelies, the King Penguins' eggs and chicks of the King Penguins are also not safe from their enemies, the Skua Gulls and Giant Petrels or Fulmars, commonly called "Stinkers," who nest just above their rookeries. Therefore, they must be guarded carefully by their parents.

Since King Penguins do not have to migrate, they can take their time about such important matters as breeding and moulting. All year long bands of Kings may be seen fishing together, always on the lookout for the Leopard Seal, which feeds along these South Georgia shores — on penguins whenever possible.

While the King Penguins and their relatives are the undisputed bird owners of South Georgia Island the year round, there are countless thousands of other sea birds which are attracted to this part of the world by the plentiful food supply in the sea. They make use of this and other islands for breeding purposes for a very short time in the Antarctic summer. The albatrosses, many of the petrels, and the shags, to name only a few, add their beauty and voices to the island life for a little while. Sooner or later, they move out to sea but return again each year.

Every ship, whether a whaler, explorer or your own imaginary one, that comes near South Georgia is met by the beautiful blue-black bird considerably larger than a crow and called by the whalers the "Blue-eyed Shag." This large King Shag, as it is also known, flies so close alongside the ship's lookout that a man might easily reach out and catch it. A brilliant blue ring around its bright eyes accounts for its descriptive name, but the bright orange wattle between its eyes and beak, in contrast to the black back and pure white throat and belly, is just as striking.

No longer a fit, but worth a try anyway!

Having welcomed the ship or satisfied their own curiosity, the shags fly back to continue the building of their steep-sided, cone-shaped nests on the top of dead tussock clumps. Mixed with the activity of nest building, they do much curtseying and what seem to be cheek-to-cheek minuets, with all the grace of a dance. The males take short joyous flights, then return to their love-making and helping the females in the nest building.

When all is ready, the female King Shag lays two or occasionally

51

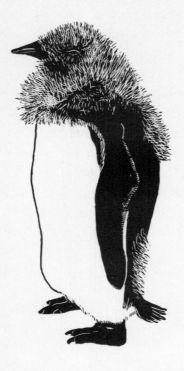

Still part baby. In his new suit he will look like his parents and can then enter the water and feed as they do.

three eggs in the nest and the pair take turns keeping the eggs warm. The sitting bird will not fly off the nest, no matter how near you come, but she will twist and turn and snap at you and make a loud, retching noise!

Besides the penguins and shags, we find that a number of different kinds of petrels have adopted the island, each living and breeding in its own particular way. Some are found beneath the shag nests, in the tussock clumps where they find protection for their eggs by burrowing in the root-bound dirt of the same plant. One species of these, the Shoemaker Petrels (also called Cape Hens), often arrives when the ground is still frozen hard, and then they are forced to use old burrows or raise their young in ice-caves. If they are late and the ground is soaked with melted snow-water, they use their beaks to dig the dirt loose and then scratch out the earth, much as a dog would do. They pull the stubborn tussock roots away, working with great energy for short periods. Then they fly up onto the tussock grass and preen their feathers and chatter and rest before they begin digging again. They seem to enjoy the activity, but it takes time for each pair of Cape Hens to make a six-inch wide tunnel six feet long, with a circular room a foot across at the end. In the center of this they scratch the dirt into a mound, leaving a gutter around the sides to let the water run off. A great deal of bird energy goes into hiding the single pointed egg. By this time the nursery is apt to be a mud hole and perhaps the birds would prefer to be in an ice-cave, after all.

The Diving Petrels also live in burrows and, in order to be safe from the Skua Gull and the "Stinker," leave their homes only at dusk to fly to the ocean feeding grounds. These dainty little birds use their wings for swimming, much as penguins do. They fly through the water as if it were air, and dive through air as though it were water.

There are other penguins on the island. Here we see left to right a Macaroni, three Gentoos and a Rockhopper.

The King Shag

When their hunger is satisfied, they return to their burrows — each entrance is under a stone — and follow the twisting and turning tunnels to the nests which are situated under stones. The poor Diving Petrel chick may have only the bare ground for a bed, but at least it has a stone roof over its head!

The Whale Bird, another burrowing petrel, is the most numerous of the birds that breed on the island. They fly from their burrows at dusk and settle lightly on the surface of the sea. With their wings folded and with only their feet pulling them through the water, they scoop up the small sea animals and plants, called plankton, letting the water drain off through their saw-like gills. This manner of eating is much like some kinds of whale, and because of this the blue-gray bird gets the name of Whale Bird. A dark gray stripe through the eyes gives the creature a smiling expression. Whalers call it by still another name, that of Fire Bird, because dazzled by the light of their fire, the bird seems drawn toward it and is often destroyed in the flame.

Then there are acres of small dusty-black birds, known as Wilson's Petrels, with white rumps and white bars on their wings, hovering over the surface of the water, dipping the tips of their toes in the sea as if walking on water. Perhaps if you listen carefully you can hear their soft courting whispers at the entrance of their burrows — for they, too, have chosen the safety of the underground to raise their young.

About the middle of October, the chattering of the Cape Pigeon, another petrel, fills the air with throaty cries throughout the day and night. These petrels build their nests high on the cliffs so that they can spring into the air easily. On land, they are clumsy and unable to stand, but once on the wing, they glide gracefully above the surface of the water, scooping up food and allowing the water to run out of their mouths in the same manner as the Whale Birds. When a couple of Cape Pigeons have finished building their nest, the pair fly away to sea for a ten-day "honeymoon" before returning to take up the duties of housekeeping.

While all these petrels fear the skuas, they have even more to fear from the Giant Petrels, rightly called "Stinkers," because of their

Shoemaker Petrel sits at the entrance of her burrow beneath tussock grass.

bad tempers and filthy habits. These build their nests high up above the other nesting birds and are always ready to swoop down and steal unguarded eggs or chicks — almost without losing a beat of their wings.

These large, bloodthirsty birds vary in color from brown to white, and their feathers have a most untidy appearance. A ridge of feathers above the eyes causes the birds to appear to be wearing a frown. The "Stinker" is ungainly and awkward when it lights on the ice or the shore. The bird cannot even keep its balance unless its wings are half open, and after taking a few steps has to sit down and rest. But once in the air, the "Stinker" is a strong flyer, with great speed, while the wing beats seem to have a peculiar creaking sound, as if the joints were rusty and needed oiling. Actually, this noise comes from air being forced through the throat and nostrils as the chest muscles contract.

The nests are built where the strongest winds blow, so that the birds can have the advantage of them in taking to their wings. Into a tussock root and seaweed nest, each female lays a single egg and the pair incubate it for six weeks. The newly-hatched baby chick is ugly, shapeless, covered with long, fluffy down, and has a huge beak. Like all petrels, the babies spit up when disturbed and soon the rookery is dirty and smelly, as well as the noisiest place on the island, for the "Stinkers" scream continually. The skua can easily steal an egg or young chick, for the "Stinker" parents are slow and clumsy and too stupid to cover their babies quickly.

The chicks grow fast and by Christmas they are the size of chickens, very fat, and covered with long, curly gray down. By February, they have moulted and wear new black plumage. When April comes, the parents, still living up to their name, "Stinkers," do not return to feed the young, who remain unwatched and unfed on the nests. Finally, the chicks get so tired of sitting that they simply have to move about and start beating their wings. Hunger forces them to take their first flight to the water's edge, where they soon find that they, too, can catch squid.

Like their parents, they fear nothing, and if you really happened to be on the island they would swoop at you, circle above your head,

Cape Pigeon rests on the water.

The "Stinker" is hated and feared by all birds.

dive at you and pull out of the dive just in front of your face, giving you a sharp blow on the head with their wings, or a strong peck with their beaks.

It does seem too bad for the other sea birds to have this ogre bird and the Skua Gull added to the hardships of the severe weather conditions which they have to put up with while trying to raise their young, doesn't it?

The Albatross,
Master of the Winds

If any bird has mastered the winds forever blowing around the Antarctic continent, it is the albatross, the bird with the greatest wing spread in all the world!

Most of the year the albatrosses sail on motionless wings round and round the continent at the bottom of the world. Perhaps they, next to the penguins, can lay claim to these most southerly seas. Except to raise their young, they never leave the cold waters but fish for squid there day and night.

Sailors on vessels that enter these southern waters, especially those on sailing ships, keep a sharp lookout for the albatross, for they have an old superstition connected with this beautiful bird.

The albatross will appear out of the sky and glide about twenty feet above the after-sail. Poised there as though motionless, looking to one side and then the other, it seems to inspect the spar. The bird then circles away a short distance and returns, this time to look over the topmast stay. It then sweeps forward where, except for its head and eyes, which turn as if to see everything, the bird keeps stationary with scarcely a movement of the wings.

Some of the sailors believe that each albatross contains the soul of a drowned mate and that he is looking over all the ship's lines, to

The albatross sails on motionless wings round and round the continent at the bottom of the world.

make sure that they are clear for running and will not foul if pulled in a hurry. It is good luck to have this guard inspect the ship, but it is bad luck to kill one! So the sailors watch a following albatross with special interest and never cease to marvel at the way it hangs motionless above the ship, like a kite on a string. The large bird can let down a foot and bring it forward to scratch its head, or turn and peck at a misplaced feather without moving its great outstretched wings.

This is the Sooty Albatross, one of many albatrosses that circle about the icebergs and islands. The bird wears smoky-gray plumage, and about each black eye is a narrow ring of white feathers, broken only in front of the lower lid. This makes the eyes appear to stare and adds to the impression that the bird is really searching.

Like all the other albatrosses the Sooty uses the islands for a brief time for nesting, but unlike the others it chooses cliffs for its brief home.

Each pair of Sooties selects a place for a nest, high up on a steep cliff. Other Sooty nests are quite close and their shrill cries can be heard echoing from cliff to cliff. Into her mud nest each female lays a single beautiful white egg with a ring of red speckles near one end. While one parent sets on the egg, the other sails above in all kinds of weather, occasionally flying close to its nest and gazing at its mate as it passes. The baby chick spends the first few months "clinging to its cradle," as sailors say. If it didn't "cling" it would surely fall off the cliff. The legs of the albatross are nearly helpless and are rarely used, so their choice of a nest is such that they need only to face the wind and dive. The babies have no chance to make test flights. Their first must be successful or they will be dashed to pieces on the rocks below.

Another kind of albatross is the Mollymawk, about the size of a goose. They come to the island shores in countless thousands and crowd together in rookeries on the long, tussock-covered slopes at the foot of the high crags on which the Sooties nest.

There are two kinds of Mollymawks and these differ only in looks. The White Molly or Black-browed Albatross is pretty well described by the two names given to it. The black feathers above the eyes give the bird a stern expression. The other is the Blue Molly, named for the blue-gray of its head and back. Yet looks must be important to the two kinds of Mollies, for they live in separate rookeries, in spite of all their similarities.

The cock Molly gathers a beakful of mud or bits of tussock and brings it to the waiting hen. He drops his bundle, bows and makes a low braying noise. His mate bows back and then arranges the mud in the nest and packs it down with her webbed feet. They nibble at

The albatross seems to inspect the spar.

Sooty Albatrosses build their nests high up on a steep cliff.

each other's necks, bow low and bray again before the cock goes off for more nesting materials. All the Mollies in the rookery carry on this courting ritual but not at the same time. In October, the handsome egg is laid, and both birds take turns sitting on it until the chick hatches, and indeed until the young bird is half grown. After this the chick is left unprotected while both parents go fishing. If the young albatross is disturbed, it defends itself by squirting a red oil at the intruder; but if left alone, the chick just shuffles about in its nest, snapping its beak and making a soft, crying sound.

On the west end of South Georgia, in the most exposed places where the furious winds never stop blowing, the largest birds that fly — the Wandering Albatrosses — have their rookeries. In the bright sunshine, the sea and sky are a cold blue and the icebergs gleam white. The tussocks on the slopes of the island are a dull green and among the plants may be seen the white breasts of hundreds of brooding albatross hens. A loud and continual chorus of braying and honking is carried far by the fierce winds and echoes and re-echoes from the cliffs.

The albatross, one of the most impressive birds alive, has a wing spread of eleven feet. An old bird may be pure white, except for the long black flight feathers on the under wing. The plumage changes with age and the chick that starts nearly black ends up nearly white.

In the winter, the snow on the slope lies deep, but every spring it melts into pools and riverlets. As soon as the snow-line retreats up the mountainside, the albatrosses return to build their nests of tussock roots and mud. The steep hillside is the next place to a cliff, for the albatross then has a long downhill run to help it rise from the ground. The cock brings the nesting materials. In his ungraceful, waddling way, he goes again and again for additional mud or roots, until the nest is three feet high and three feet across. The bird is built for flying, however, not walking. His center of gravity is so far back that, in order to keep his balance, he must stretch his head low down in front and wave it from side to side at every step.

In the courting ritual, as with the Mollies, there is much nibbling and bowing and "talking." Sometimes the pairs take part in a dance, facing each other, bowing and sidestepping in a circle, while at the same time moving their heads from side to side. The cock opens his eleven-foot pair of wings, with the tips held over his head. From time to time, with his bill pointed skyward, he gives a loud cry. All over the rookery, mated couples perform this same dance. They remind us of an orchestra playing together without a director.

The courtship of the Wandering Albatrosses lasts a long time but at the end each pair has in its nest a large, fragile egg weighing about a pound. From then on they take turns brooding it. The egg

Black-browed Albatrosses

The courting 'dance' of the Wandering Albatross

stays warm, enfolded in the breast feathers, while the sitter spends much of the time bending over the edge of the nest, scraping up the wet soil around the base and plastering the steep sides. These soon become increasingly smooth and finished-looking. At other times, with its head tucked in the soft back feathers, the bird appears to doze.

The eyes and ears of the Wandering Albatross are always on the alert and when a skua or "Stinker" flies overhead the bird gives a warning gabble. There is one very queer thing about the Albatross rookery: the nests of the "Stinkers" are very close by. You would think the albatrosses would be afraid to have their nests so near their enemy, wouldn't you? The answer probably lies in the fact that the "Stinker" does not feed close to its own nest and so the nearer the albatrosses get to the "Stinker" nests, the safer they are.

Sometimes one albatross sets for days without relief while the other parent ranges far off shore, fishing. Again the change is often made every four hours. But the birds are good parents, and when the chick hatches, they feed it well with krill and squid and fish. The Wandering Albatross chick grows very fast and becomes very fat, which is just as well, for when the cold winter comes, the parents desert their young chick and fly away to soar above and all around the South Polar lands.

The young bird sits in its nest for three months or more, alone, unprotected and unfed, while the winter blizzards rage all about. There it squats on the nest in the dark and uses its blubber for heat and energy. This is the nearest thing to hibernation to be found in the bird world. Since the chick has grown black feathers under its down, however, at least it has on warm winter underwear!

Poor baby albatross! It must feel abandoned in the world, yet there is other bird life about it. Besides the penguins, the little titlark or Antarctic Pipit spends the winter as well as the summer on South

The Wandering Albatross has the longest wing span of any bird.

Georgia. Life is hard on the small birds but at least they can get out of the worst winds by hiding behind a boulder, while the young Wandering Albatrosses sit on the most exposed headland, with the ice and snow blowing about them. All through the bitter, dark, cold winter, their fat is slowly changed into bone and muscle, as well as heat, so when summer comes again, many are ready to climb off their nests and try their legs and wings. Hungry as they are, they must first strengthen their wings, and so they stand on the hillside by their nests, facing the wind and spreading out their long wings. They beat their wings and spring off the ground again and again, and in this way learn to fly until, finally, most of the young have left the old rookery.

Somehow the old birds manage to return to the same rookeries year after year. If they find any young albatrosses still "clinging to their cradles," they get the nests cleared in short order, for this is a new summer and nests must be repaired or even rebuilt. The ejected young, all dressed up in their dark suits, sit back on their heels, with their toes turned up, looking as if they would topple over any minute. They snap their bills like their parents and gabble and cackle and thus add their noises to the bedlam of the rookery. Meanwhile, they wait for the urge or ability to make the first flight to find the food they have never been taught to catch in a sea they have never even seen.

Seals

One by one, the female Elephant Seals climb out of the water until the beaches are crowded with animals waiting for the birth of their pups. All winter, the seals have been far out at sea, no one knows where, for they do not even come to the land to sleep. Yet with each approach of the Antarctic summer, thousands come to the islands around the Southern Continent which they use briefly as breeding grounds.

Within a week of their arrival, the pups, wearing black wooly fur coats, are born. Their eyes, eyelids and lips are also black, and their queer little noses are soft as silk. The pup looks small beside the thousand-pound, ten-foot-long mother, but it is only by comparison, since even the baby weighs one hundred pounds or more at birth!

All through the week of waiting for the birth of the pups, the bull Elephant Seals also arrive, but they stay at a distance and do not come near the cows until after the pups are born. Shall we have a look at an enormous bull asleep on the edge of the snow, just out of reach of the tide? His fur coat is dull brown, coarse, harsh and of no value commercially, for no one would want a fur coat made of such stiff fur. But this sixteen-foot creature is very fat and his blubber is used in making oils. Because of this, he is never safe on land and it seems a shame that he has to come to the shore at all. But he is here now to round up a harem and, while he waits, he sleeps, with his chin on the snow and his flippers tucked under his body.

The most unusual part of the great Elephant Seal is his long, flabby nose, which hangs down in front of his face as far as his mouth. It is this nose that gives him his name, but he can't make use of it as the elephant does his trunk. He can't even raise it! Apart from size, the bull looks like the cows on the beach — but we have come too close, and he is disturbed! He puts his flippers on the snow at his side and raises his great scarred chest. As he throws his head back, he opens his mouth, takes in a deep breath and lets it out in a long, loud, bellowing roar. He stands fully eight feet tall, with about one-third of his body still on the ground, his nose blown up in a great round swelling. Then he drops down and lunges away from us, with his back rising and falling and his thick blubber rippling under his skin.

After the pups are born, each bull gathers as many cows and their young as he is able to defend into a group called a harem. The largest and strongest, of course, have the largest harems, while the youngest bulls and the late arrivals may have to remain bachelors — or they may at any time steal an unguarded female.

The bull that we watched sleeping has managed to secure several females and their wooly pups. The cows roar almost as loudly as the bulls, and the babies cry all the time they are not sleeping. In the harem the cows and pups lie close together, with a wide space separating the group from another equally well guarded harem. The bull, with his eyes for the moment on a neighbor who has come too close, turns to discover that an unattached male has entered his harem, so he goes into battle with a loud bellow. He not only looks furious, he attacks fiercely. Both bulls rear to their full heights on their flippers and tails and sway face to face, roaring and lunging forward, each trying to gash the neck and shoulders of the other with his tusks.

They dodge, break away and lunge again. With blood streaming down his neck, the weaker and younger bachelor backs away, with the old bull seal biting at his shoulders as he retreats toward the outer edge of the colony. However, the victorious seal cannot follow far, for he must return to guard his harem before another bull takes advantage of his absence and tries to take over his family.

Family life is not peaceful, as you can see, for as the bulls fight and roar, the cows cry in answer to the pup's bark. Yet there is another and a more peaceful side to this harem life. From the time the single pup is born until he is weaned, the cow seal never leaves her offspring — not even to eat. If the baby wanders away from her side for a second, she answers his frantic calling cry with a shrill one of her own and hurries after him. She sniffs and nuzzles the little black wooly baby as she rolls on her side to nurse it. If it has trouble finding the teats, she hitches forward to help and even uses her flippers to push the young seal to the right place for feeding. The pup sucks noisily and greedily on one teat and then on the other. After about five minutes, its stomach is filled and the sleepy baby cuddles close to the mother's side. It is small wonder that the pup grows so fast, for the milk is very rich — about half of it is pure fat. Actually, the baby puts on weight faster than it seems to grow, for after three weeks, when weaning takes place, the pup is only a foot longer than at birth but it is three hundred pounds heavier. A thick layer of blubber has been laid down under the baby's skin.

By October, the Elephant Seal pup starts to change his black coat. First, he loses the wool on his back and belly and finally on his face and head, leaving a sleek coat of light gray hair, soft as silk. By November, dressed in their new fur and fully weaned, all the young seals gather in a large herd near the shore, where they quarrel and play in and out of the water and sleep for long periods on the beach. They are too plump to move about easily, so they just loaf for a month

Bull Elephant Seal guards his harem. His noise doesn't disturb the nursing pup in the background.

or six weeks, living on their stored-up fat.

The breeding season is hard on the adult Elephant Seals and, after the pups are weaned, the harems break up. One by one, the old seals go back to sea, to feed again on squid and to let their battle scars heal. For a few months, the young pups are alone on the island, in and out of the water, safe for the most part, unless there is a Leopard Seal hiding in the kelp beds, waiting to attack them.

By March, which is the beginning of winter in the southern hemisphere, the old Elephant Seals return to the islands and old and young herd together on the beaches. The old seals are now in good condition, covered with thick blubber and ready to fast while they moult their hair. The seals need warmer coats to spend the winter months in the cold seas, although the young seals keep their gray coats through the first winter. Now is the time when the old Elephant

Seals make their way back from the beaches to the deep channels or ditches made by melting snow between the tussock clumps. Here they wallow in the mud and rub against the tussock roots, to help rid themselves of their old, matted coats. When they appear again on the beaches, they are sleek and smooth and ready for a winter in the icy waters.

The cows and pups leave the beaches of the islands first. By the middle of April, all the bulls have followed and the loud roars of the Elephant Seals are stilled during the gloomy winter months.

Fur Seals, Sea Lions and Leopard Seals also use the South Georgia shores for breeding but not as they did some time ago. The poor Fur Seals were doomed from the time man first saw them. Soft fur could be sold to make coats for the ladies in London and Paris, so millions of Fur Seals were killed on this island alone. Today, the Fur Seals are protected by international treaties and once again they are beginning to appear on the beaches in the breeding season.

From a distance you cannot distinguish the Fur Seal from the Sea Lion, for they are the same size and both are smaller than the Elephant Seal. The Sea Lion's coat is lighter, however, and, fortunately for the owner, the fur is harsh and of no commercial value. Both the Sea Lion and the Fur Seal use their flippers like legs and they seem to gallop rather than hitch along over the rocks. Indeed, they can move faster than a man can run and they are able to climb steep rock ledges as well. Several hundred Fur Seals and Sea Lions sun themselves on the rocky ledges seventy feet or more above the sea. They leap into the sea when disturbed and then bob up to the surface to look you over.

Each bull Fur Seal guards a large harem of from thirty to one hundred females. The bulls fight hard for the right of ownership. The baby seals are born within a few hours after the cows arrive on the beaches, and one cannot help but wonder at the close timing of the

Fur Seals sun themselves on the rocky ledges high above the sea.

two events. The cows go back to the sea to feed and leave the pups in nurseries. When a mother returns to nurse her black baby, she is able to pick her own from a mass of quarrelling, snapping and crying pups, apparently with no trouble at all. The mother remains away for longer and longer periods until her baby is weaned. When the pup is about a month or six weeks old, it learns to swim and soon swims away with its mother.

Almost rivaling the Killer Whale as the villain of Antarctica, the Leopard Seal, or Sea Leopard, swims near the edges of the ice floes, hiding in the kelp, if there is any, waiting for an unsuspecting penguin to come too near. Sometimes the seal even leaps out of the water to snatch a bird standing near the edge of the ice. At other times, it often comes to the surface with a large fish in its enormous jaws, swallows it with one gulp, looks about, takes a deep breath and dives again.

When the Leopard Seal comes up on the ice or onto the shore, the animal approaches the edge at full speed and shoots out of the water. This seal looks different from other seals. Leopard-like spots are responsible for the name, that and the fact that this seal hunts as viciously as a leopard. Its head and neck are all one and there seems to be more of the animal in front of the flippers than is the case in other seals. Its long neck and large mouth with sharp teeth, plus the manner in which the seal wiggles across the land or ice, holding its flippers close to the ten-foot body, and pressing first the chest and then the back region to the ground, combine to make the Leopard Seal a fearsome sight. This animal leads a solitary life. It hunts alone, sleeps alone on one side, with flippers folded on the chest, and the cow even comes all by herself to shore to have her pup. The baby Leopard Seals are not ferocious until they have been weaned. Then they are ready to fight, and when they are old enough to slip into the water with their mothers they soon strike fear into the hearts of all the other animals around the island or on the ice floes where they hunt.

The Sea of Whales

As the long Antarctic night comes to an end and each day grows longer, the great whales arrive. Their large, curved backs break surface as they roll over or dive among the icebergs, their spray shooting high into the air. The whales, the largest mammals known on land or in the sea, arrive in schools or herds or singly after a long migration of hundreds of miles from the warmer waters around the coasts of the continents to the north, where they had journeyed to spend the winter. For some unknown reason, no matter how far away they wander, they swim back to familiar feeding waters in the summer.

The greatest concentration of whales is in the Scotian Sea, often called the Sea of Whales, for this deep ocean, enclosed in an arc of islands extending from South America to the Antarctic, is the real home of the whales. Here and elsewhere around the South Polar Continent, where the strong winds blow the pack ice toward warmer waters, is found the earth's richest pasture composed of minute plant food which is absent on the continent itself. These one-celled plants and the tiny animals that feed upon them are called plankton. They are so dense that the water resembles thick soup. The krill, a small, shrimp-like animal, eats the fine plankton, and the largest of all living mammals — indeed the largest creature that has ever lived — the Blue Whale, a hundred feet long, feeds on the tiny krill.

The Blue Whales, the Fin Whales, and the Humpback Whales all belong to a class called the whalebone whales; that is, they have great sieves called baleens hanging in their mouths. Each of these wonderful strainers is made up of about three hundred grayish plates with coarse bristles on the inner edges, and each plate may be as long as forty-two inches. Altogether, they form a most efficient straining mechanism for gathering great quantities of krill as the whales swim through the rich waters with their mouths open.

The Blue Whales, the largest animals in the world today, are named for their mottled bluish-gray skin, with white flecks on the undersurfaces. They swim about in schools of twenty or more, always keeping within a few yards of one another. Once they were very plentiful in these icy waters, but not any more, not since man dis-

Whalebone whales

covered that each Blue Whale produced as much whale oil as two Fin Whales or two and one-half Humpbacks.

The Fin Whales are slightly smaller than the Blue Whales, being only about eighty-five feet long. They arrive in the Antarctic waters a little later than their immense relatives, but they come for the same reason — to feed. The plain bluish-gray back coloring extends farther down on the left undersurface than on the right flank — one can't help but wonder why!

The Humpback Whales, about fifty feet long, have stouter bodies than the other whalebone whales. Their color is interesting, too, black above and white below, with the white areas marked with black and the dark areas marked with white. They also have numerous grooves on the underside, between the flippers. These whales go to the coastal water farther north in order to mate. Although attracted by the plentiful food, they return to the Sea of Whales each summer.

The Sea of Whales contains other whales besides those that have whalebone sieves to strain out the little shrimp-like krill. These are the Killer Whales and Sperm Whales, both of them toothed whales. The Killer Whale is the enemy of all the larger animals of the sea, even of the large Blue Whales. They hunt in packs, like wolves, and are the most vicious of the animals of Antarctica, tearing at their larger relatives and gulping whole the penguin, seal or porpoise unfortunate enough to be near. They are boldly marked in black and white, may be thirty feet long, and have exceptionally large, strong teeth. The tremendous, shark-like dorsal fin that rises five feet above the water as they break surface makes them recognizable from far off. Packs of Killers often swim under the ice, and when they discover a shadow overhead, they strike the ice with their backs, shattering it and spilling the poor, unsuspecting creature that caused the shadow into the sea to be devoured. Sometimes the Killers even stick their heads six or more feet out of the water in order to look around on the ice for more penguins and seals.

The Sperm Whales are also found in Polar waters, although they do not normally live here. Those that venture so far south are probably males that have come because of the abundance of their favorite food, the squid. The most characteristic thing about this large black or brown toothed whale is its gigantic head, which takes up one-third of the total length. Within the head is a tank holding as much as five hundred gallons of Sperm Whale oil, which is highly prized.

All of these whales — Blue, Fin, Humpback, Sperm and Killer — are mammals, just as you are and as such, just like you, they have warm blood, breathe air with lungs and bring forth living young and suckle them with milk. Most whales even have a few hairs on their chins, a reminder that once upon a time — many millions of years ago — their ancestors had hairy coats. Once they must have walked on land, but they have long since evolved streamlined bodies like fish. They have changed their forelegs into flippers, losing their hind legs altogether. Their once pointed tails have now become wide, driving propellers.

Thus equipped, they can travel with ease through the cold water, their blubber holding in the body heat. This stored-up fat is important to the whale, for it not only keeps the animal warm in the cold waters, but serves as a protection against heat as well when the whales go into tropical waters, which they must do to bear their young. The blubber is also a source of food, stored up for use on the long migration north, for the whales eat nothing during the many months they are away from the polar regions. When they return each summer, they are thin; and it is only after eating the rich food of the Antarctic waters that they regain their thick, oily coats of blubber fat.

Whales must come to the surface to breathe every few minutes, usually every five or ten minutes; but they may stay down as long as

Forty-foot Killer Whales hunt in packs like wolves.

forty-five minutes when necessary. When they surface, they force the air out of their blow-holes (two in the whalebone whales and one in the toothed whales) with so much force that it can be heard from a distance. The mist air particles can be seen a long way off. The whale is then said to be "spouting," and it really does look like a fountain of water. The whale inhales fresh air and then sinks horizontally, repeating this procedure several times, showing only the part of the head with the blow-holes above the surface, until all the air in the lungs is changed. When the lungs are full, the back of the whale usually may be seen arched high as the animal "sounds" or dives. The Humpback and Sperm Whales throw their tails above the surface as they sound and sometimes even leap completely clear of the water. It is from the particular manner of such sounding and blowing that whalers distinguish the different kinds of whales from a distance.

Each year, whaling ships follow the whales into these southern waters, to kill the animals for their oil. A whale weighing seventy tons will yield thirty tons of blubber and two tons of oil. Before man learned to produce vegetable oils, whales were the only means of supply and his greed has already killed off all the whales in certain waters. We can only hope that controls can be enforced before this happens everywhere to the largest mammals in the world.

Just as the whaling ships leave the Antarctic waters before the long night sets in, so do the whales. All summer they have eaten and grown fat, and now they swim northward to warmer waters, to give birth to their young, which the females have carried from ten to twelve months. Their migration routes are well known. For instance, the Humpbacks that feed far to the south of South Africa swim north to Madagascar, while those from far south of Australia go north to the Australian coast. All move to places where conditions are best for producing and nursing their calves.

A single baby whale is born to one mother, and it may be as long as twenty feet at birth. The baby is suckled, like all mammals, for the first part of its newborn life. Whales live entirely in the sea, and do not come to shore even to give birth to their babies, so it is difficult to study their young. We do know, however, that whales produce young every two years.

With the approach of summer they start south to the same old feeding grounds where the young, now thirty-five to forty feet long, are weaned on krill. The young whales become adults after two or three years, and they are full-grown at four to five years, an amazingly rapid rate. Whalebone whales come south because of the small shrimp-like krill, Killer Whales come because the whalebones do, and all find food in abundance in this rich pasture of Antarctic seas.

So our long imaginary trip comes to an end and it is time for us to see something of the real journeys that men have made to the frozen continent at the bottom of the world.

Discovering Antarctica

The people who drew maps in the fifteen and sixteen hundreds sketched in an imaginary continent to the south of the known world, yet no one had ever really proved that this land existed. Many sailing ships had been caught in the strong winds and had been driven southward into the ice seas, but the men aboard had seen no land. By 1750, there was a growing doubt as to whether a southern continent really existed. But the age of discovery was not over, and in 1773 Captain James Cook, a celebrated English navigator, sailed southward to explore the Antarctic regions and to decide the question once and for all. He crossed the Antarctic Circle time and time again, probing as far south as possible into the ice-filled waters. He discovered the high, snow-covered island of South Georgia and took possession of it in the name of His Britannic Majesty and his heirs forever. How strange the volley of muskets fired on this occasion must have sounded to the inhabitants of the island — the seals and penguins and other birds!

Captain Cook returned to England, convinced that there was a southern continent but that, because of the ice, it was impossible to reach the land, and so it could therefore be of no economic value. However, he brought back stories about the "sea of whales" their ship had sailed through and the thousands of seals on the icy shores. This was enough to set the stage for the second interest in the frozen south. Where there were whales, there was oil, and seals meant fur. During the next fifty years, many ships crossed the Antarctic Circle, in search of suitable places to catch whales and seals. Many of the adventurers discovered new lands and left their names on places which we can now find on the map of Antarctica.

By 1835, many countries were interested in this new region that was bringing wealth to those who sought oil and fur. A new scientific interest in studying the Polar regions began with France, the United States and Great Britain, with all three planning expeditions and building ships especially constructed to navigate in ice-filled seas.

A Frenchman, named Dumont d'Urville, while searching for the Magnetic Pole, give his wife's name "Adelie" to the ice-bound coast and also to the small friendly occupants, the penguins, he found there.

It was the American, Charles Wilkes, who in 1840 really came across the first proof that land lay below all the vast ice and snow they encountered, and it was from the Emperor Penguin that he got his proof. How fitting that the real emperor of the frozen continent should offer the evidence for the existence of his kingdom. Wilkes found a quantity of black pebbles in an Emperor Penguin's stomach. Pebbles meant that land could not be far away, so he quickly sought and discovered it and gave his name to that particular section of the Antarctic continent.

An Englishman, Captain James Ross, who had already visited the Arctic and located the North Magnetic Pole, sailed in 1840 in search of the South Magnetic Pole. The ice prevented him from reaching the Pole, but his two ships, the *Erebus* and the *Terror,* sailed along the coastline for five hundred miles and penetrated deep into the Antarctic — as far as eight hundred miles beyond the Antarctic Circle. He saw a mountain belching flame and smoke and named this active volcano *Erebus,* after one of his ships, while to an extinct volcano near by he give the name of *Mount Terror.* He sailed on to discover a cliff of ice which rose from two to three hundred feet out of the water and extended unbroken for two hundred and fifty miles along the coast. Ross had broken through the ice pack into a sea never seen before and had discovered the great Ice Barrier. His ships had sailed to within 12° of the South Pole.

All of the ships in the South Polar region not actually engaged in whaling now carried on board groups of enthusiastic scientists who were interested in everything about the frozen Antarctic lands and seas and who made collections of all the marine and bird life they could obtain. The Captain of one ship even gave up his quarters to house the growing collection. On one occasion, a young scientist on one of Captain Ross's vessels was so excited over a skin of the Emperor Penguin that he jumped down the main hatch with it in his hand at the very moment the Captain was coming up. But the skin survived, to be carried proudly back to England. This was the first specimen of these strange birds to be seen outside Antarctica.

It was a Norwegian crew aboard a whaler at the turn of the century who first set foot on Antarctica. About the same time, Englishmen aboard the *Discovery,* under Commander Robert Scott and accompanied by Ernest Shackleton and Dr. E. A. Wilson, made a trip south to study Antarctica during a long, dark winter. They set up a base and traveled with dog-drawn sledges the whole length of the great Ice Barrier to the foot of Beardmore Glacier, and thus discovered the most likely route to the South Pole, although they did not then attempt the journey. After the dark, cold winter had ended and they prepared to return to England, they found their ship held captive by the pack ice and had to spend a second winter huddled at the foot of Mount Erebus and Mount Terror. These volcanos, they discovered, were on islands close to the mainland but not a part of it. Against these mountains the barrier ice piled high with the pressure of the greatest glacier of the world behind it. Here the party lived through another winter with Emperor Penguins as their nearest neighbors, so at least they learned a great deal about these interesting friendly birds.

But Germany was not to be outdone and she also sent scientists southward. They reached the Ice Barrier and skirted it, and along the way their thin ship also became frozen in for the long winter. The land nearest them they named for their emperor — Kaiser Wilhelm II.

A little later, a group of Swedish scientists almost lost their lives when the boat sent to pick them up after a winter of study on an island in the Weddell Sea was lost in a fierce storm. At the last minute the Swedes were rescued by an Argentine gunboat. During these years, with science as the motive, many countries took part in the discovery and study of this great frozen land far to the south of us.

Out of this period of discovery some of the most thrilling true adventure stories have come down to us. You will read them yourself some day, I hope, and to guide you I have listed some of the books about them at the end of this chapter. Here I can only hope to introduce you to those men whose names will always stand for the highest courage and achievement — men who gave their lives in the adventurous exploration of a new continent.

In 1908, Ernest Shackleton had his ship towed by a steamer as far south as the Antarctic Circle in order to save coal. On his ship he had some unusual passengers. They were ponies — to draw his sledges over the ice in place of dogs. They did not prove as satisfactory as dogs in traveling over ice, but Shackleton did succeed in climbing Mount Erebus and he also explored farther along the way to the South Pole.

It remained for Captain Robert Scott to reach the South Pole, although he lost his life in doing so; and when he did arrive at the Pole, he found the tent left a month before by a Norwegian named Amundsen. In 1911, the *Fram*, Amundsen's ship, was scheduled to explore the Arctic when in great secrecy it suddenly headed south, stopping nowhere. On reaching Antarctica, four men on skis, with fifty-two dogs drawing sledges, made their dash to the Pole and back. Nothing was added to scientific study by this accomplishment, however. It is the story of the journey made by Scott and his party that comes to us as one of the greatest true adventure tales ever told.

While waiting for a suitable time to make the journey to the South Pole, a side trip was made by Dr. E. A. Wilson, H. R. Bowers and A. Cherry-Garrard — a trip to secure Emperor Penguin eggs for scientific study. Cherry-Garrard has told of that journey to collect the penguin eggs in a book called *The Worst Journey in the World*. These three men spent five weeks in frozen clothes at temperatures of 60° below zero and colder, in a winter night which did not end, with only the light of the stars to guide them. Because of dangerous crevices or cracks in the ice, each step forward in the dark had to be an experimental one. Getting around these crevices often meant traveling ten miles to advance forward three. During one of the worst storms they progressed over the ice no more than two miles in eight hours. Finally, with ropes and ice axes, they made the descent in the dark to the Cape Crozier penguin rookery and secured five eggs. Two were crushed in falls, but three frozen Emperor eggs were brought back to England to be studied, after the worst journey in the world.

When the long night ended and summer light returned to the Antarctic, Scott and his South Pole party were ready to start for the Pole. They followed the route that Shackleton had explored earlier — only this time they had motor sledges, as well as ponies and dogs. Soon the motors broke down and had to be abandoned. Then it was discovered that the ponies could not stand the cold, and so they had to be shot. Finally, after a sixty-seven-day march through a continuous blizzard, Scott and four men reached the South Pole, only to discover that Amundsen had been there thirty-four days earlier. They

Map of Antarctic discovery

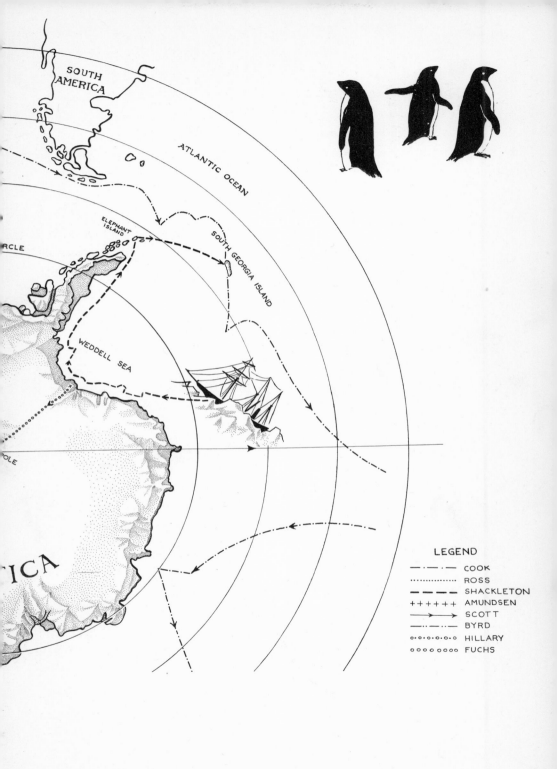

SOUTH
AMERICA

ATLANTIC OCEAN

ELEPHANT
ISLAND

SOUTH GEORGIA ISLAND

RCLE

WEDDELL SEA

POLE

ICA

LEGEND

— · — · — COOK
· · · · · · · · ROSS
— — — — SHACKLETON
+ + + + + AMUNDSEN
————→ SCOTT
— — · — · — BYRD
o·o·o·o·o·o·o HILLARY
o o o o o o o o FUCHS

were disappointed and tired, but they started on their return journey through weather worse than they had ever dreamed possible. First, Seaman Evans broke down and died. Then L. E. G. Oates, who was injured, walked away to die rather than delay the party. Finally, Scott, Wilson and Bowers ran out of food and fuel oil and froze to death in their tent. Their bodies and their diaries were found in 1912. Theirs is a story of bravery that will never die.

There is another exciting story of exploration in Antarctica — that made in 1914 by Shackleton. On this trip, he planned to cross the continent from the Weddell Sea to the Ross Sea, by way of the South Pole. His first disaster came when his ship, the *Endurance*, was crushed by ice and had to be abandoned. The twenty-eight men in the party camped on an ice-sheet, which moved northward for four hundred and fifty-seven days and finally broke up in 1916, forcing the party to take to their three small boats in the roughest seas possible. After six days in open rowboats, they all landed on Elephant Island. Shackleton and five men took the largest boat, which was twenty-two feet long, and sailed to South Georgia Island. They landed on the south shore and left a sick man in the shelter of a cave, while Shackleton and the others climbed the ice-covered mountain of South Georgia and reached a whaling post on the north shore — a feat never repeated and unbelievably difficult to accomplish. But Shackleton did secure help and returned to pick up all his men, the sick man as well as the others who had lived on seaweed and limpets and had found shelter under the two small boats. Isn't that a story to match any adventure you've ever heard?

In 1929, Richard Byrd made the first of his five Antarctic expeditions. The airplane was a part of his equipment, and in November, 1929, he left "Little America," his base in Antarctica, and flew over the South Pole. From the airplane it was now possible for the first time to map the Southern Continent. On each visit to Antarctica,

Byrd added to the already growing knowledge of the new land; and one long, dark winter he spent alone at his base, making weather observations as well as gathering other scientific data.

When asked why he kept going back to Antarctica, Byrd replied, "I like it there. I like the endless reaches of wind-rippled snow, the stark peaks, the awesome glaciers . . . I like the symbols of life's triumph in a lifeless land: the squawking Skua Gulls, the comical penguins, seals wheezing at their blowholes, the arching back of whales."

The International Geophysical Year of 1957-58 was a co-operative effort by scientific groups from sixty-seven nations to study, at the same time, all over the world, the nature of weather, magnetism, glaciers, gravity, winds, and such matter. To make these investigations, scientific stations were set up from the North to the South Pole and around the Equator, and expeditions to Antarctica were a very important part of the whole project.

Richard Byrd lived to set up "Operation Deepfreeze," as the Antarctic part of the world-wide scientific study was called. After his death in March, 1957, Dr. Paul A. Siple carried on. No one could have been better qualified, for he had not only accompanied the noted explorer on all five of his Antarctic trips, but was a nineteen-year-old Eagle Scout when he made the first trip south with Byrd in 1928.

Eleven countries set up bases on the South Polar continent and the near-by islands. Only two parties, both in 1911-1912, had previously set foot at the South Pole itself; but, in 1957, tractors, hammers, saws and the like were flown in and soon shattered the Pole's chilly silence as a base was built to house American scientists. Britain, France, Russia, Norway, Australia, New Zealand, Argentina, Chile, South Africa, Belgium, and Japan all carried out similar Antarctic studies in other regions. This, the first evidence of widespread cooperation between the scientists of the world, as they studied and shared their findings, has made the International Geophysical Year (or IGY, as it was called) important to us all.

Early in January, 1958, Edmund Hillary, conqueror of Mount Everest, and three companions made a dash of twelve hundred miles by tractor from the Ross Sea to the South Pole. Starting from the other side of the continent, Dr. Vivian Fuchs and his party, stopping every thirty miles to make important scientific observations in spite of extremely bad weather conditions, reached the South Pole a little later the same month. After a short rest, they pushed on, for their purpose was to cross the continent, a twenty-one hundred mile journey, perhaps the most difficult undertaking of any IGY group, without a break in their scientific observations.

Antarctica remains a challenge to explorers and scientists alike, for the great white continent holds a wealth of secrets concerning the nature of the earth, and will keep many of them for a long time to come; the vast stretches of ice, the bitter cold and the long, dark winters will continue to defy the efforts of all but the strongest and bravest men.

Who owns Antarctica? Certain countries, of course, staked claims by way of exploration, but such claims have to be backed up by permanent occupation. When we remember the two hundred mile per hour gusts of wind and the temperatures that drop to one hundred degrees below zero, it is hard to imagine a permanent settlement, with schools, stores, and churches, any place on the continent. Scientific stations, yes, can easily be imagined, but the Emperor Penguin will continue to be the undisputed "ruler" of Antarctica for many years to come.

Suggested Reading List

The South Pole	R. Amundsen
Exploring with Byrd	R. E. Byrd
The Worst Journey in the World	A. Cherry-Garrard
The Voyage Toward the South Pole	James Cook
South with Scott	E. R. G. R. Evans
Scott's Last Expedition (Scott's Diary)	L. Huxley
Voyage to the Southern Seas	James Ross
The Voyage of the *Discovery*	R. F. Scott
Heart of the Antarctic	E. H. Shackleton
South	E. H. Shackleton

Index